Welfare Gutter Rats

Jo Hammers
Paranormal Crossroads & Publishing

Welfare Gutter Rats

Copyright © 2016 by Jo Hammers

All rights reserved. No part of this book may be reproduced or transmitted in any form or by any means without written permission of the author. For information, address Paranormal Crossroads & Publishing, Po Box 5056, Bella Vista, AR 72714.

ISBN 978-0-9911540-3-6

www.paranormalcrossroads.com

This work is fiction. All of the characters, organizations, and events portrayed in this novel are either products of the author's imagination or are used fictitiously.

The publisher does not have any control over and does not assume responsibility for author or third-party Web sites or their contents.

The scanning, uploading, and distribution of this book via the Internet, or via any other means without permission of the publisher is illegal and punishable by law. Please purchase only authorized electronic editions and do not participate in or encourage electronic piracy of copyrighted materials. Your support of the author's rights is appreciated.

Cover Art by Jo Hammers, 2016.

Table of Contents

1. Are Welfare Gutter Rats Dark Beings?   5
2. Light Being Others Who Cross Over to Darkness   7
3. Get a Job? I Will Lose my Food Stamps   9
4. Dollars to Panhandlers   10
5. Paradise Builders   12
6. Blaming Others for Welfare States   14
7. Parents Who Choose to Rear Children in Life's Gutters   16
8. Rats Neglect Teaching Their Children Skills   19
9. Handling Over Your Dollar Bills to Panhandlers   22
10. Fat as a Cat Female Panhandler   24
11. Wheel Chair Panhandler   26
12. A Poor Working Human in Not a Gutter Rat   29
13. Flattened Biscuits   32
14. Dark Forces are Looking for New Prey   34

CHAPTER ONE

Are Welfare Gutter Rats Dark Beings?

Two types of souls enter Earth life and travel for lifetimes in human flesh. Light being souls are from the upper heavens/God/Divine Essence, and come to Earth on missions or for educational experiences. They are workers and students. Christ and Buddha were light being souls.

You will not find light being souls on welfare rolls. Light being souls are goal setters and achievers. They live and breathe to better themselves, as well as the social conditions for their families and other light beings about them. They turn their faces from darkness, or the gutters of Earth life.

Dark soul beings enter Earth life from a dark womb, or dark hole in the universe. Human brain thinking has nicknamed that place 'Hell'. Dark beings make choices in Earth life to rape and plunder anything that they have not had to work to produce. They are con-artists and abusers, ones who take advantage of others, welfare systems, and charities for dollars and items that they do not have to work for. Thieves are dark beings, as are lifetime or long term welfare and faker disability recipients.

Dark beings, or devils in human flesh, use and abuse welfare, charities, food stamp programs, food banks, clothing banks, etc. in order to not have to work for the finances to feed, clothe, and shelter themselves. They will milk welfare, neighbors, family, friends, and charity systems for every free thing they can get, even if they don't want or need it. Dark beings (long term welfare recipients) are sociopath rapists. Their prey is charities and welfare systems. I call them

'Welfare Gutter Rats'.

Welfare Gutter Rats are mostly female. Male Gutter Rats usually choose to be street corner panhandlers. A third type of gutter rat exits. It is the faker who rapes the government for a disability check.

There is no welfare in the heavens of light. All orbs or souls of light are equal and all work for their energy and light. There are no free-be handouts. Welfare gutter rats and pan handlers are dark beings. They will not go to life in the heavens when their human bodies die. They will return as souls to the dark womb or 'Hell' from whence they have come. There is no salvation for devils. Salvation or rescue by masters like Christ is for light beings that have lost their way on Earth.

Saviors are light being rescuers who restore or return lost light beings to their paths or point them toward the portal light to home. They do not save sociopath dark beings. Christ told Satan to get behind him. He didn't save him!

You will know whether souls are dark or light beings by whether they choose to work or take long term from society. Anyone receiving welfare or other types of assistance for more than a couple of months, instead of filling out job applications, is a dark soul male or female gutter rat. Light beings will always be looking for a job and have goals that will take them out of the gutters of life and off welfare rolls. They will also pay back with interest to charities, family, friends, etc. what they have needed to ask for when temporarily needing help.

I do not believe in enabling, feeding, or housing Gutter Rats or street corner Panhandler Gutter Rats. I am a light being. I do not embrace devils in human flesh.

CHAPTER TWO

Light Being Mothers who Cross Over to Darkness

Light being souls are mini gods in human flesh. Because of their divinity, they will never be happy living in low income housing or ghettos on Earth. They enter Earth life from the paradises of the heavens. When in human flesh on Earth, light being souls will create mini paradises of what they are used to living in the heavens.

A Native American is capable of building a T-pee or Hogan wherever he is. An Eskimo is capable of building an igloo. Light beings coming to Earth will build paradises, or Garden of Eden dwellings and experiences.

There are light being mothers who cross over to the dark side. Perhaps they choose to waste their lives in drug addictions, alcoholism, gutter living, prostitution, etc. Just as there are traitor soldiers in time of war, there are traitors to the light.

Free will choice can be used or abused by souls coming to Earth. Free will choice is a learning experience course that must be mastered or failed. Should a light being soul be born to a drug addicted, alcoholic prostitute of a mother, it will eventually abandon her, and her dark lifestyle choices. When a newborn's human body reaches maturity, it will walk away from dark parents, never looking back.

Some runaway children and adults, those who disappear, are simply light beings who have walked away from darkness. Light beings do not see the need to embrace or keep in touch with family beings that are dark demon 'Gutter Rats'. Souls of the light are at war with darkness, not embracers of it.

CHAPTER THREE

Get a Job? I will loose my Food Stamps!

Demon dark beings coming to Earth revel in sponging off of freebee systems, so they don't have to work and create. They are users and con-artists, that choose to live in low income housing and other ghetto and gutter apartment hells because they do not have to work and pay for them. If you offer a Gutter Rat a chance for a job to get him or her out of the ghettos and gutters, he or she will undoubtedly say, "I can't do that! I will lose my food stamps and free government housing."

Any human making the above statement is a dark being, a user of welfare, charities, food stamps, and other freebee housing systems.

CHAPTER FOUR

Dollars to Panhandlers

Light being souls work and create on Earth, just as they do in the heavens. Long term welfare gutter rats and street corner pan handlers are dark souls. You should not embrace darkness in any form. If you embrace/support a dark devil, you automatically turn your own light into a shade of gray. Embracing darkness is being a traitor to the light.

If you give a dollar to a dark soul panhandler, you are a traitor to the armed forces of the light. If you give clothing to a dark soul, you are a traitor. If you work in a soup kitchen feeding devils, you are a traitor. If you give food to food banks that give to devils, enabling them to not have to work for their daily bread, you are a traitor. If you shelter to a dark soul, you are a traitor.

Charity starts at home. That means, give to light being causes only. Gutter rats, repeat panhandlers, and disability fakers are not light beings. Charities created to feed, clothe, and give shelter to those who will not work are set up by dark beings. Darkness takes care of its own, just as light beings should take care of their own.

Before you give a dollar to a panhandler on the street that you do not know, offer him a job mowing your lawn, cleaning out your garage, or doing other odd jobs for the day at minimum wage per hour. He will probably curse you and tell you that he makes more money standing on his corner begging and conning people than what you are offering him. If he accepts your job offer, it is okay to help him. Willingness to work separates those of darkness and those of the light. That does not mean that he might not be a shade of gray light being that is suffering Karma for some misdeed he has done. His circumstances may be a Karma whack. Don't embrace his grayness and take him home. His Karma is his Karma. Give him a few dollars and move on. You don't want to be in trouble with Divine Essence/God for interfering with circumstance punishments.

CHAPTER FIVE

Paradise Builders

My twelve year old grandson has always loved Leggy blocks. He especially likes putting together the city buildings. He now owns and has erected most of the building block structures available. So, he has had to choose something different to ask for at birthdays and other holidays. On his last birthday, he asked for a Leggy Chess set. My grandson is the builder and playful creator god in his pre-teen world. He lives and breathes blocks and the game of chess.

As adults, you and I are types of him. We take what we have, (our money and talents) and create block type homes and playful recreation hobbies to be the creator/god of.

When entering adulthood and the job force at eighteen, I dreamed of building and living in a little Ozark Mountain Cabin and having a separate small building to write and create art in. Writing and Art were my passions, just as blocks and chess are my grandson's passions. I worked, saved, and now have built my dream. I own a little Ozark Mountain Cabin and have a separate building to write and paint in. It is my heaven on Earth.

Light beings will labor and create personal shelters and play worlds to relax in. Dark soul beings will rape others, charities, and shelters for housing and relaxation. Low income housing is shelter not worked for, as are apartments and housing paid for by welfare systems. A dark soul stealing and using your bike, gaming system, or boat is his taking and using items that he has not labored and worked for. A thief (non laborer) is a dark soul. If you have a repetitive thief in your family, walk away from him. He is not a light being. Human biology does not make light and dark beings family.

If you are reading this, I sincerely hope you are not a 'Gutter Rat'. My wish for you is that you get the wheels of your thinking process turning and use your divine thoughts to create a personal heaven experience. You have free will choice. Whatever you can think, you can create! Thoughts become things, when acted upon. Don't think welfare applications and gutter living. Think and take steps toward working and creating a 'Heaven on Earth' living experience. Save and create an owned home for yourself! Afterward, move on to create a chess set play experience to go with it.

Welfare, food stamps, and charity handouts create hells on Earth. Drinking, drugs, over eating, hanging out in gangs, etc. are not Chess play experiences. Dark recreations will chain you to nothingness and eventually destroy you.

CHAPTER SIX

Blaming Others for Welfare States

Women complain that they can't escape their welfare states, or that it is someone else's fault that they and their children are where they are in life. Not so! To begin with, a woman chooses the man she wants to be with, as well as to have children by him. Even if she has a child from being raped, she makes the decision to keep or give it away. She also chooses to work or not work. Our lives are the result of our wise or unwise yesterday choices. We are the god or devil in our lives.

'Complaining' and 'blaming others' women could have chosen in their youth to remain single and have no children. They could have chosen an education, instead of chasing fantasy knights in shining armor. Their current welfare state of living is the result of their yesterday choices and not filling out job applications.

If a woman chooses a lowlife, abusive, lazy couch potato criminal for a mate, it is her choice. However, when her dark being man dumps her, she is faced with having to deal with the fallout from her yesterday choice, as well as having to make new choices. She can spend a day filling out applications for employment, or filling out a welfare application. She can remain single or choose another knight in shining armor nut case. What her future holds will depend on her now choices. She is not the victim of others. She is the victim of her own choices. Her children are the victims of her yesterday choices.

Marry a violent man, you will get beat. Choose to have three kids by a couch potato and you will be responsible for working and making them a living. Marry a pervert and you will share him with his perversions and contract diseases. Marry a truck driver; he will never be around on a consistent basis for you or your kids. Marry a drug addict, he will eventually approach and hook one of your children or family members to drugs. What you choose in life will one day come back to bless you, or bite you in the butt. You are your choices, and will live the results of your choices. You are absolutely responsible for your current lifestyle. It is the result of your yesterday choices. Don't blame others for your bad decisions!

The first step to escaping a welfare 'Gutter Rat' state is to return to the point where you started. Take a good look at your first adult decisions. Then wisely choose not to make the same choices now. Run from knights in shining armor. Adopt out children that you are unwilling to work and support, or cannot feed. Love is sometimes letting children go on to better situations. Decide to not live in the gutters of life. Get a job. Create a future. There is no future, or home ownership, in welfare living or in the ghetto apartments and gutters of life. Don't blame others. You are your yesterday's choices. However, you can choose differently for your tomorrows.

CHAPTER SEVEN

Parents Who Choose to Rear Children in Life's Gutters

Some women and men just don't want to work and better themselves, unless life forces them to do so. They want an easy way out. Wanting a free living is a characteristic of a dark soul being. Using and conning systems, friends, family, food banks, and other social services are dark deeds. They also want a savior who will provide them a free back door into heaven.

Salvation or rescuing is for lost light beings, not con-artists and lazy couch potato dark beings. The Christians have it all wrong. They try to save the satanic, devilish, dark forces in the gutters of life and on welfare rolls. Christ told Satan to get behind him. He didn't save him! Salvation is simply the rescuing of light being souls that have lost their way, or have fallen off their spiritual paths. Rescuers, or saviors, point them back to the light and portals to home in the heavens.

At death, con-artist devils return to their own dark heaven which is referred to as 'Hell'. There is no light being rescuing, salvation, or freebee tickets to the heavens of light for them. Salvation preachers are some of the worst embracers and enablers of dark welfare, non-working for their daily bread 'Panhandlers' and 'Gutter Rats' there is. Salvation preachers welcome in and enable darkness to sit on pews they have not helped to pay for, instead of casting dark devils out of their sanctuaries. Lost light beings are those who have strayed from their religious/spiritual paths. They are not thieves, rapists, murderers, gutter rats, drug addicts, alcoholics, and other types of sociopath devils.

There is free will choice on Earth. Both light and dark beings have that power. Children of the light are intent on working and making good lives for themselves, and their children. They will choose home ownership, educations, and being all they can be in their communities and churches. A dark being will be intent on not working and raising his or her children on the streets and in the freebee gutter charities of life.

Welfare parents choose to live year after year in the gutters of life. They also make other bottom basement choices. Not going to mosque, church, temple, or synagogue is one. They choose not to attend, when doing so would let their children associate with those of higher classes. Choosing to stay home on Sunday and barbecue for all the gutter and ghetto low life drug dealers will not provide children with opportunities or role models. Welfare parents choose to send their children to ghetto schools. They could choose to home school them in order to give them a safe quality education. After all, 'stay at home' welfare parents have the time to go to church for every service and invest their time in their children's education. However, down deep, they are only interested in their food stamps and checks, not what is best for their children.

Lower than welfare choosing parents are those who choose to take their food stamps and sell them to fund their alcoholism and drug addictions. There are gutters in life, and then below it are the pits of hell. Some parents willfully choose to rear, abuse, and starve their children in subcultures below welfare gutter life. There is hell, and then there are the bottomless pits of hell.

There are basics in life that we have to have to survive. We need water to drink food, clothing, a place to bathe, and a place to sleep. When worlds come crashing down, humans find themselves in the position of having to make choices to fill those needs. There are always two options. One will be a wise choice and one will not be.

Where you are in life right now is the result of your yesterday choices and no one else's. If you don't like where you are, turn from your errors and make new choices so your tomorrows will be what you want them to be.

Turning from past choices and making new ones must be done by female gutter rats and panhandling gutter rats if they want better lives. The same goes for those on disability. A disability check is a crutch, not success. Those who fake aches and pains for disability checks are dark beings looking for freebee lifestyles.

Without welfare freebees as an option, complaining welfare state women would make one of two choices. They would choose to fill out job applications, or they would join forces with the drug dealers and other low life, con-artist individuals in the gutters, raping those about them. Devils don't change. They just move on to other cons that will provide them a free living.

We are our choices in life. Karma returns to us according to what our choices are. Christians say we reap what we sow! I say we deem ourselves light or dark by what we choose.

CHAPTER EIGHT

Rats Neglect Teaching Their Children Skills

My twelve year old grandson asked me to take him to the Library. He was out of reading material. I immediately added it to my schedule. Whatever my grandson needs to be successful and further his individual path, I make every effort to provide, as does his parents. My grandson is an avid reader, on a swim team, loves to cook, and is a boy scout. We are providing multiple opportunities for him to explore, so he can become all that he can be. That is what good parents and good grand parents do.

Last weekend, a distant niece and her two sons (7 & 8) came for a visit. Our family got together and planned a pool party to entertain them. To our horror, neither boy had ever been to a pool or had learned to swim. They were reluctant to get in the 4 inches of water in the kiddie pool. Their mother tried to brush off their non-swimming status by stating that they were into fishing and hunting, not swimming.

A child who goes fishing needs to be able to swim! It was my opinion the boys had never seen a fishing bank. If they were truly little fishermen, they would not have screamed in fear of putting their feet in the kiddie pool water. I knew my distant niece was lying about the fishing, to save face for having not taken them swimming till now.

In my opinion, my niece probably pawned her two boys off onto some boyfriend or neighbor who was a hunter, and did hunt occasionally. However, the two boys openly talked about shooting birds, squirrels, rabbits, stray cats, and anything else that moved just for sport. They were not hunters for meat.

It is my opinion that allowing boys to hunt and kill small animals for sport is setting them up to become future, gun toting criminals who will move on to shoot bigger prey such as humans. The mother was okay with letting them kill birds, squirrels, stray cats and dogs, rabbits, etc. The two little boys openly talked about using anything that moved for target practice. I was appalled. Too my dismay, my distant niece is a dark, welfare 'Gutter Rat' type, and is teaching her boys to be the same.

As I sat in horror watching and listening to my two distant nephews, I recalled a conversation with my brother who said he had visited the niece several times in the past year. He confided in me that there was never food in her refrigerator for her little two boys, but there were always cartons of cigarettes and full ash trays on her kitchen table.

A dark soul welfare gutter rat will choose cigarettes over food for her children. She will sell her food stamps for drugs and alcohol. She will waste money given her for utility bills, and then hit up charities with sob stories of why she can't pay them. A welfare gutter rat will only think about herself. A welfare gutter rat will buy cigarettes and beer instead of food for her children.

Souls enter Earth life and travel in human bodies for transportation. I am a soul and so are you. Both dark and light being souls travel in human forms. Too my dismay, I have a niece who is a dark being gutter rat, and she is subjecting her two children to hunger, guns, violence, and denying them opportunities like going to church and learning to swim.

I am pro adoption. I believe that welfare mothers should be given 60 days to get out, get a job, and provide for their children. If they don't do it, in my opinion, their children should be adopted out to good homes that can provide for them. The same should go for those mothers claiming bad backs and disabilities. You would be surprised how many women would get miraculously well if their welfare, disability checks, and food stamps stopped!

I also feel that children of divorce should be awarded to whichever parent works and is capable of providing the best lifestyle for them. In my opinion, welfare gutter rats shouldn't be given custody of children at all.

Abusive, dark soul gutter rat parents deny children opportunities for growth and becoming. Welfare gutter rat mothers cage their children up in ghetto apartments, in order to collect checks and food stamps on them. Gutter living is all the children will ever know, till they are old enough to walk away and abandon their gutter rat mothers, if they live to see that day.

CHAPTER NINE

Handing Over Your Dollar Bills to Panhandlers

Panhandlers routinely standing on street corners are dark beings, as are those continuously standing in welfare, food stamp, and charity lines. Dark being, devil panhandlers want to use and abuse the workers of society. They will be more than glad to take the hard earned dollars (you hand out car windows to them), to keep from working themselves. Only the naïve stop, roll their windows down, and fork over free dollars to drug addicted, alcohol drinking, con-artist street bums/panhandlers. Supporting darkness is turning from God's light.

We of the light are at war with darkness, not embracers of it. Do not give to any charity that enables dark ones to survive a single day without working. Be aware that you are supporting the forces of darkness when you roll down your car window and hand over a dollar bill to a man standing on a street corner begging. There are shelters for men as well as women. Non-worker individuals, who continuously rape shelters and free soup kitchen food, are dark devil souls. They are 'Street Gutter Rats'.

I like to write early mornings while I eat my breakfast in fast food restaurants. Recently, traveling for business, I frequented a single fast food restaurant near where I was staying for several weeks. The restaurant was on a very busy corner and panhandlers were out every morning working it like crazy. After a week of watching them thru the restaurant's window, I came to recognize the regulars who were holding up signs reading homeless and hungry. I also watched those same regulars enter the restaurant after morning rush hour. They would order the most expensive items on the breakfast menu board, while the regular working stiffs who came in ordered from the dollar menu. They were eating better than the conned working men who were handing them out dollars from their car windows.

I decided to strike up a conversation with one that I had seen working the corner for at least three weeks. He also was used to seeing me in there, and may have thought I was homeless. The man told me that he had been panhandling for 21 years and was from New Jersey. He also confided to me that he made more money in his couple of rush hours panhandling than he could ever possibly make out on a job. He also told me that he had saved his panhandling money and had bought himself a beach house in Mexico, where he intended to retire a couple years down the road. He said he would occasionally fly down to Mexico and spend a week or so in his beach house, when the weather was bad in the states. To look at him, you wouldn't think he had a cent to his name. He had on dirty tattered clothing and played the part of a homeless bum with an 'I am homeless and hungry' sign quite successfully. Do you have a beach house in Mexico? Have you rolled down your car window and helped a panhandler buy one, unknowingly?

CHAPTER TEN

Fat as a Cat Female Panhandler

The big city I was born in is plagued with panhandlers on every corner, especially on the weekends or social security day when people get paid. When you are in business and out and about every day, you come to recognize the regulars, month after month supposedly 'hungry and homeless'. They are actually professional con-artists who fleece the public. Yesterday, seated in a lawn chair at the entrance of the supercenter, a huge 300 or more pounds bleached blonde woman sat holding up a sign reading . . . 'HUNGRY . . . ANYTHING WILL HELP!' I snickered. If you weigh 300 pounds, have the money to bleach your hair blonde, and sit smoking expensive cigarettes; you are not hungry. The obese woman had probably eaten herself into her fat state on food stamps, pan-handled money, and food bank freebees.

I pulled into a discreet spot in the super center's parking and watched the woman for awhile. When rush hour was over, a male panhandler, her age, came walking over from an opposite corner. After gathering up her chair and belongings, they made their way to a brand new red utility vehicle that was hidden amongst the supercenter's customer's cars. Average working Joes in old dented and dinged cars had stopped on a regular basis handing them hard earned dollars. The woman wasn't hungry, homeless, or in need. I watched her take off her dirty panhandler jacket and put on clean clothing before getting into her spotless car. The pair had been conning the public.

Shaking my head, I exited my car and entered the super center to make a few grocery purchases for the weekend. Inside, I ran into a professor friend. I told him about the male and female con-artists who were panhandling out at the stop light. He laughed and told me about a police report he had recently read. A woman's car had been broken into. Stolen was a newly purchased designer handbag and designer brand clothing valued at three thousand dollars. Also stolen were her food stamps.

If there are truly hungry people, charity food banks will give them several bags of groceries, as well as a hot meal. Those standing on street corners with hungry signs are usually con-artists. They are 'Street Gutter Rats', just as public assistance con-artists are Welfare Gutter Rats. 'Disability Faking Gutter Rats' are a third variety.

It is my opinion that food stamps should be just a 30 day program, or done away with entirely. The food stamp program encourages the gutter rats of our society to not work and abuse/con the light beings of our society who do work.

I am thankful I have open eyes to see the con-artists that are plaguing city streets across the United States. Con-artist panhandlers are dark beings traveling in human flesh. They are not of the light. We should not enable darkness by giving them a single dollar of our hard earned money. If we do, we turn ourselves a shade of gray.

CHAPTER ELEVEN

Wheelchair Panhandler

Recently, due to controversial stories about a wheel chair man panhandling on the state line of Arkansas and Missouri. I decided to drive there and spend a week of mornings secretly watching that location. I had been told that regular beggars, not one-timers, were working a particular corner as you turned into a super store there.

I arrived at the state line location about seven in the morning. I actually live two hours away in one of the major cities. Not having breakfast yet, I decided to run quickly into the superstore to get a cold drink and a donut to snack on while I watched the corner. Inside, a professional man in a business suit and tie smiled at me flirtingly and said good morning as I shopped. I returned the greeting and continued my snack shopping, ignoring him. In my thinking, he was probably a banker or a lawyer. He was well groomed and the tie read professional. I checked out a few steps behind him, after watching him pay for three plastic grocery bags of various items. One of the items was a dozen glazed donuts.

After paying for my couple of snack items, I left the store walking at a short distance behind him. I eyed his backside. He looked great in his suit and tailored pants. He did not turn to see that I was behind him and watching him. He walked out into the parking lot to his vehicle. My vehicle was parked a double row of cars behind him, facing him. Up to that point, it was my opinion that he had possibly been killing time in the super center before going to his office somewhere. I also assumed that he was possibly supplying the donuts and juice for his office crew for the morning.

As I unlocked and seated myself in my vehicle, my cell phone rang. I answered it. An acquaintance called to tell me a long winded tale about what had happened in her world the night before. Listening to it prevented me from leaving my parking spot to park closer to the corner to watch the panhandlers there for the morning. As I listened to my friend's tale, I watched the neatly dressed professional man store his three sacks of items in his car trunk. After putting his last sack into his vehicle's trunk, my curiosity was aroused as he removed a wheel chair from the trunk of his auto. He then opened it up, and sat down in it.

"What the heck . . . ?" I muttered to myself.

The man then proceeded to take off an artificial leg. Afterward, he pulled his pant leg up as high as he could get it above his knee, bearing his knee and the area where his leg had been amputated. He then changed from his clean business suit jacket into a dirty rag of a jacket, and then removed a well worn cardboard beggars' sign from his trunk before closing it. In shock, I watched him roll himself in the chair to the corner, where he held up his tattered sign that read, 'Hungry, Broke, Homeless! Please help!" Keep in mind that he had just purchased a dozen glazed donuts and juice, as well as other items. The donuts weren't even off the second day old, mark down rack.

I hung up on my friend, started my vehicle, and pulled up to where I had a view of him for the morning as he panhandled. He worked the two rush hours in that area like a pro. Hard working Joes, children, and old women stopped and gave him dollars and miscellaneous items of food they had just purchased at the superstore for themselves. When he left, after rush hour, he left behind the cheap items he did not want. He then rolled back to his auto, put his leg back on, stood up, and took off the dirty jacket. He then put the wheelchair back in his car trunk, his business suit jacket on, and then drove away.

For a week, I made a point of parking in the rows near the corner of his choice to see if he was pulling the con on a regular basis. He was. Every morning he arrived in his expensive car, nicer than I was driving. (I drive a 2015 Chevy Colorado). He would go in the superstore to shop, and then come out, get his wheel chair out, and repeat the taking off of his artificial leg and then performing his leg cut off hungry act with his cardboard sign. It was very apparent that he was making himself a pretty good living, making people feel sorry for him due to his missing leg.

Also, each morning I made a point to watch him at a distance on his shopping jaunts inside the store, prior to panhandling. He walked around in the supercenter like he was the cock of the walk, eyeing and flirting with register girls and women customers. There is no telling what con he was trying secretly to pull as a side line with the women he was flirting with on the inside of the store. Con-artist men like to move in with and use working women for free housing, utilities, bodily needs, etc. In his business suit and flirting, the panhandler was definitely eye candy. Hooking and making prey of women in some way, could have been another con game he was running on the side.

Charity dollars and other items such as food should be given to where you absolutely know they are going to someone who needs them. I feel it is better to pick out a 'working family' that is experiencing hardships for some reason (in your circle of friends), to give your charity dollars or food to.

When you give blindly to food banks, clothing banks, soup kitchens, shelters, etc., you really do not know who is benefitting from your good will. If you feed, clothe, and shelter a dark con artist individual, you are enabling him to live and prey for another day on the blind innocent.

Charity starts at home. Give to those in your social circle who are in need. Do not give to dark being welfare gutter rats or panhandling male con-artists who will not work for their daily bread.

If welfare and food stamps were done away with in the United States and begging be made a felony, you would be surprised at how many panhandlers, disability fakers, and welfare gutter rats would enter the work force when they got hungry enough.

Con-artists, both male and female, are sociopath dark forces or demons in human flesh. God says to flee darkness, not embrace it.

CHAPTER TWELVE

A Poor Working Human is not a Gutter Rat

What is a welfare gutter rat? It is an individual who willfully chooses to live on welfare, food stamps, and charity handouts. Man has freewill choice. He can just as easily fill out a job application as a welfare one. Gutter rats want free rides at the public's expense. If you were to offer them a job, they would say, "I can't do that. I would lose my welfare and food stamps." Freebees in life are more important to them than being successful, contributors to society.

A female welfare gutter rat is like a pack rat. She takes and takes and takes. She does not create for herself or give to society.

A poor working woman or man is not a gutter rat. There is a difference between being a poor worker and being one who chooses not to work, but takes from society. A poor person with light being integrity tries to work and find a way out of his poverty. He has goals.

Finding the way out of poverty is as simple as checking out some books from the library about handling your finances, investing, and finding the job that is right for you and your talents.

Recently, I was reading a short article written by an Arkansas woman at Christmas time who decided she would help her poor, single, working mother neighbor, who had nothing to give her child for Christmas. Her working neighbor mother was totally opposed to receiving charity. However, she was a poor working mom who was barely making it. She decided to go to a food bank to ask for a Christmas basket for her neighbor mom, and possibly a Christmas toy or so for her child.

She arrived at the charity place at 8:00 A.M. and stood in line for an hour and a half till she made it to the door to enter and apply for her neighbor friend. Nearing the door, she was appalled at the comments of those coming out of the charity complaining about the boxes of macaroni and cheese and other cheap staple items they had been given instead of what they expected of more expensive items, such as canned hams, turkeys, etc. They also complained about the dollar store type donated toys given them for their children. One threw the toys in the trash outside the building.

The good intentioned neighbor was totally appalled. She was equally disgusted as she watched those in line wearing high end, name brand shoes and carrying designer handbags. She then started to watch the newer vehicles that possibly 75 per cent of those receiving freebees were leaving driving late model newer cars. It was at that point in time that she realized that charity starts at home and should be given to those you truly know are in need. Her eyes were opened to see that charity was not giving blindly to programs that gave to the con artists and charity rapists of society.

Even though the good neighbor was near the head of the line (after an hour and a half of standing) she left the line with a new perspective. She also decided she could afford to buy a couple of sacks of groceries for her neighbor as well as a nice gift for her neighbor's child. She also decided that she would no longer support charity food and clothing banks that were enabling the con artists of society to live on freebees. She decided she would make sure that her charity dollars went to a working family who truly needed it and would appreciate it. She would no longer give her charity dollars blindly. In an hour and a half, standing in line moment, she came to the reality that there is a difference between charity rapists and the truly poor in the United States. The truly poor are those who refuse to take charity and are determined to make it by working.

After reading this story, I personally went and parked at a food bank and watched those coming and going on hand out days for a couple of months. She was right. I watched a lot of designer shoes go in and then those wearing them come out complaining about their 'macaroni and cheese' type freebees. I also watched them drive off in almost new cars after lighting up cigarettes. If a man or woman can afford cigarettes, they can afford to take the same money and purchase food for themselves and their children for the day.

Choice is the fine line dividing those of darkness and those of the light. A poor light being will fill out a job application, instead of a welfare application. A dark being will fill out welfare applications and multiple food and clothing bank forms to keep from working.

CHAPTER THIRTEEN

Flattened Biscuits

My daughter takes an ordinary, generic brand, can of biscuits and turns them into morning sweet rolls. She starts by flattening the little round biscuits out. Then, she puts a teaspoon of chocolate chips on them, rolls them up, butters the tops, and then bakes them. After baking, they look like tiny crescent or cinnamon rolls, and are morning divine!

Human life has its flattened biscuit moments. Losing a job and our only source of income is one of those moments. What we do with our flattened situation is up to us.

Getting in a welfare or food stamp line is someone giving up and ignoring their possibilities as flattened biscuits. Selling your hat for money for gas to get to a job interview is the sweetening of a flattened moment with chocolate chips.

Man has free will choice. What he chooses to create in his flatted moments, deem him special or a life-discard. Man can change himself from one thing to another. Free will choice gives him that power. If a hobby of ceramics doesn't work for you, reinvent yourself and pursue a hobby of new possibilities, such as photography. If an occupation as a house painter doesn't seem exciting enough, pursue a career in trucking or taxi driving. When we feel flat in our lives, we have the free will choice to spice up our life moments a bit. We have the choice to add chocolate chips to our flat lives.

We are like generic canned biscuits. When flattened in life, we can become low class, flat welfare gutter rats, or reinvent ourselves and become working morning sweet rolls. Flattened biscuit moments present us with an opportunity to change, re-invent ourselves, and become something that is morning divine.

CHAPTER FOURTEEN

Dark Forces are Looking for New Prey

There are dark forces as well as light forces on Earth and in the heavens. Just as there is a great womb called God that produces light being souls, there is also a dark womb that produces the total souls of darkness. There is a third group of forces. It is made up of light beings that have stepped over the fine line that divides light and dark, good and evil. The third group is light beings that have willfully turned to embrace evil. They are light being traitors and known as Shades of Gray.

People like to speak about the attacks of devils or dark forces in the gutters of life where alcoholics, drug addicts, and welfare gutter rats reside. The truth is that you are more likely to find dark forces sitting on the pews of temples, churches, mosques, etc. Why? They already have the alcoholics, drug addicts, and gutter rats in the ghettos in their clutches. They go where the holy are to try to turn more to darkness. Why waste time on the ones in the gutters that they already have?

Welfare gutter rats and panhandlers are extended arms of darkness, or the hands of Satan.

www.ingramcontent.com/pod-product-compliance
Lightning Source LLC
Chambersburg PA
CBHW061314040426
42444CB00010B/2643